PANIC IN THE PEWS

...DO *YOU* WREAK HOLY HAVOC?

Written by
Lisa Bergman

Illustrated by
Erin Bartholomew

2016

ST. AUGUSTINE ACADEMY PRESS
HOMER GLEN, ILLINOIS

First Printing December 2009
Revised and Updated January 2011
Illustrations redrawn, Epilogue added May 2016

Softcover ISBN 978-1-936639-15-1
Hardcover ISBN 978-1-936639-00-7
Library of Congress Control Number: 2011918411

For all those parents throughout history
whose children have, at one time or another,
resembled the children on these pages.

Welcome to our Church--
We sure are glad to see you.
Although we must admit
That it may be hard to *be* you.

Because, you see, our parish,
It is all made up of tykes
Whose manners during Mass
Are all too easy to dislike!

So if you want to learn just how
Good girls and boys behave,
You'd better take a lesson from
These goops who rant and rave!

Each one of them has got
A nasty habit, you might say.
So take a look and see
If *you* might be like *them* today!

Visiting Vincent just loves to be present

And see who is here (and who's not).

Though the Mass has commenced,

He's still greeting his friends--

And for Vincent, there are quite a lot!

Putting the kneeler to use as a stool

Is what Perching Percy will do--

For it seems quite obtuse

Not to put it to use,

When it gives him a much better view!

Hope you don't sit with Quarrelsome Quincy—

Each Sunday he can't seem to quit!

His talent is always to get in a scuffle

O'er *who it belongs to* and *where do I sit...*

8

Of course there are such placid boys

As Seymour Sleepyhead--

During Mass he lies about

As though he were in bed!

Then there is his sister,

The lethargic Tired Tess--

When she lies down, oh my!

You can see right up her dress!!!

Pushy Portia wants to see,

But in her way's a column;

She shoves and elbows, steps on toes--

Someone *else* should have this problem!

12

Chatty Chadwick's pleasant,

Though oblivious to those

Who wish to hear the sermon

In the place of Chadwick's prose.

14

You can oft hear Whining Warren

For he does have lots to say:

Lying on the floor he tries

To always get his way.

One who is quiet is Nibbling Nixon--

He seems to be such a good boy.

But when you look closer, you see that it's really

A *snack* that has brought him such joy.

Over here there's Lazy Lottie,

Who doesn't take to kneeling.

She rests her bottom on the pew

To relieve that *dreary* feeling.

20

In this pew over here,

    there sits a family called Bramble,

And every week, they always do

    the offertory scramble!

Crawling o'er each other,

    just as though it were a scrum,

The moment that they see

    the usher with the basket come.

22

Scribbling Susan is sure to be found

With pens and pencils and crayons around.

Doodling, coloring, writing her name--

If she's missing the Mass, well, at least she is tame!

24

Curious Curtis, he just wants to know

At *every moment* what page he should follow…

What's the priest doing? and *Where are we at?*

Barraging his parents with constant chitchat!

 26

There's Potty Prue, whose problem

Always causes such frustration:

Seems she always needs to "go"

Right during Consecration!

28

Backwards Buford faces the rear

To see what's there to see—

Forgetting that his back is turned

To Christ on Calvary.

Sullen Sally sits all slouched,

Her dress untied, hat at her feet.

Sneering and sniffling and showing her tongue,

As if to punish us with her conceit.

32

Shouting Sheldon has just one volume—

He never appears to mind

That all his protestations

Can be heard for miles behind.

Distracted Darla's docile,

But she's always off in space—

Her mind just seems to wander,

And won't stay in its place.

36

Impatient Imelda is anxious to know

How much longer till Mass will be *done?*

Asking and asking, again and again,

Can we go, because this is no fun!

Clambering Clarence climbs on the pews,

From kneeler to seat back he bounds--

His shirt comes untucked, his knees are a fright,

And his shoes send up thunderous sounds!

Frolicking Friedrich won't stay in his seat;

Like Clarence, he just can't sit still—

Off in the aisles he's dancing around,

And runs up and down as he wills.

Well, that's what it's like here—
Our cast sure is lively!
We hope you'll come visit someday.
But with all this din,
It's hard to come in—
Then come out again feeling okay!

So on second thought, we ask,
That when you go to Mass,
You look at your behavior and say:
If any of these tots
You resemble quite a lot…
If so, please make some changes right away!

For with all the gifts God gives us,

Especially His only Son,

When it's time to come and see Him, we should ask

For the gift of special grace

To behave with no disgrace,

And to put forth our best effort to the task!

EPILOGUE

It is hard to believe that seven years have passed since the early concept for this book was being worked out with the help of the teenage daughter of a close friend. Erin had a great talent for caricatures and other doodles, so when I saw what she was capable of, the idea for this book came into my head—a book that could teach proper behavior in church and have fun doing it.

Erin is in college now, and has illustrated several books for me since then. Recently I mentioned her early work on *Panic in the Pews* and she blushed. Looking back on the work of her early teenage years, I hoped she would be more proud. Later, while looking at the book, it occurred to me that she might be happier if she could have another shot at doing the drawings, now that she has more experience. When I mentioned the idea to her, she jumped at the chance.

Of course, I had to admit that I was emotionally attached to many of the original drawings, and asked her to modify them as little as possible. So past readers will still recognize most of the cast of characters within; they are simply improved a bit.

But I also wanted to take advantage of the opportunity of this reissue to visit upon a few criticisms that have been leveled at this book since it was first published. Many feel that it is judgmental. Nothing could be further from our intention! Let me explain.

The concept for this book was based on one of our family favorites, Gellett Burgess' *Goops and How to Be Them*. This delightful journey into reverse-psychology, married to complete nonsense, was also incidentally Dr. Seuss' favorite book when he was a boy. In imitating that book, we sought to poke fun at as many foibles as we could, and given that they tend to be typical childish behavior, they are of course none of them serious faults. Our end goal is not to scold "bad" behavior, but simply to hold up an ideal, with some good-natured humor, while at the same time acknowledging that no one is going to be perfect in achieving it.

We give equal fun-poking to the sort of habits that make mom want to sink into the floor, like climbing on the pews and tackling little sis to reach the offertory basket first, alongside such harmless practices as being distracted (something even we adults have trouble with) and perching on the kneeler (which, let's face it, is sometimes necessary for those unable to see over the pew rail). At the same time, we note that a handful of the behaviors found within are considered perfectly acceptable methods of keeping little ones busy and/or quiet, and of course this can help explain why we might be construed as being judgmental. For this reason, I think it is worth taking a moment to discuss why we included them as being Goop-like in nature. (Keep in mind that the Goops were made famous for such normal childlike actions as smudging windows and licking their fingers!) Most notable among these are the little girl coloring and the little boy eating.

When our children were very young, we often brought religious coloring books and activity sheets to Mass. These were all quite nice, and helpful in their way, but as our children approached First Communion age and thus were expected to start paying attention during Mass, we encountered major resistance. We realized that by trying to keep the little ones occupied with busy work (and therefore out of trouble), we were setting ourselves up for bigger problems down the road. Busy was not replaced by mature attention, it was replaced by B-O-R-E-D. And so we realized that from the earliest possible age, our children needed to be aware that Mass was Mass, and not something else. They could dislike having to be still and quiet for an hour (who doesn't?), but we wouldn't risk having them unfavorably compare Mass with Coloring Time. So are Scribbling Susan and her parents committing a Cardinal Sin? Hardly. But like the Goops' window-smooching, it will require hard work for the parent later on.

And now for the least popular topic: eating during Mass. Now, no reasonable person would suggest that nursing infants should be forced to wait until Mass is over if it happens to be feeding time. However, as no adults I know bring food to Mass, I think we can accept that there is an age at which a child needs to learn that the food must stop. This is especially true because it causes a very real disconnect with one of the teachings of the Church which is sometimes neglected today, but nevertheless remains in force: the **Eucharistic Fast**.

Since very early times, the Church laid upon her members the strict adherence to fasting before receiving Our Lord in Holy Communion, and to break this fast was considered a mortal sin. Like our Lenten observances, this fast is designed to help us deny ourselves, that we may follow Christ's exhortation to "take up our cross and follow Him." And while children too young to receive the Sacrament are of course not bound by this precept, eating during the Mass creates a great deal of confusion not only for the child who is allowed to eat and will later need to understand that this is forbidden; it also creates confusion and discomfort for those children sitting nearby who are of age, and are forced to watch other children do what they are not permitted to do.

Surely no one, with the exception at times of infants, or those who are pregnant, ill, or diabetic, should be unable to go one single hour without eating. In fact, during the Mass is a wonderful opportunity to point out to a child that Jesus was hungry and thirsty when he hung on the cross too! So if we poke fun at Nibbling Nixon, it is not an accusation of sinful gluttony, but rather it is because we hope he will learn that being hungry can be good for him—especially when the Food we can all look forward to receiving at Mass *is Christ himself.* We're sure you'll agree.

In Christ,
Lisa Bergman
Vigil of the Feast of Pentecost, 2016

Lisa Bergman is the mother of six angelic children
who never, never behave like the children in this book.
…Well…*hardly* ever…
When she's not coming up with crazy ideas for books,
she enjoys singing, sewing, cooking and reinventing the wheel.

Erin Bartholomew is currently studying art at the college level.
She enjoys fashion design, family vacations to different cities,
and her pet schnoodle Maestro!

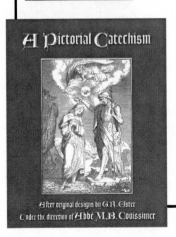

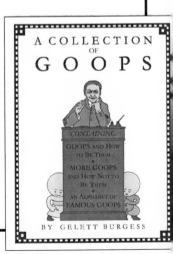

CPSIA information can be obtained
at www.ICGtesting.com
Printed in the USA
LVOW11s0807070617

537173LV00003B/13/P